PEOPLES OF THE ANCIENT WORLD

Life in Ancient Rome

Shilpa Mehta-Jones

Crabtree Publishing Company
www.crabtreebooks.com

Crabtree Publishing Company
www.crabtreebooks.com

For Lakme and Owen

Coordinating editor: Ellen Rodger
Editors: Rachel Eagen, Carrie Gleason, Adrianna Morganelli
Production coordinator: Rosie Gowsell
Production assistance: Samara Parent
Scanning technician: Arlene Arch-Wilson
Photo research: Allison Napier
Art director: Rob MacGregor

Project management assistance:
Media Projects, Inc.
Carter Smith
Pat Smith
Laura Smyth
Aimee Kraus
Michael Greenhut

Consultants: Carol U. Merriam, PhD., Chair, Department of Classics,
    Brock University

Barbara Richman, Farragut Middle School, Hastings-on-Hudson NY

Photographs: Alinari Archives/CORBIS: p. 11, p. 18; Archivo
Iconografico, S.A./CORBIS: p. 4, p. 12, p. 26; Arte & Immagini
srl/CORBIS: p. 22; Bettmann/CORBIS: p. 21, p. 23, p. 25, p. 30; Andrew
Brown; Ecoscene/CORBIS: p. 4; Burstein Collection/CORBIS: p. 8; Ric
Ergenbright/CORBIS: p. 28; Werner Forman/CORBIS: p. 25; Lindsay
Hebberd/CORBIS: p. 9, p. 24; Fotosearch/Image Source Royalty Free:
p. 18; Erich Lessing/Art Resource, NY: p. 31; Araldo de Luca/CORBIS: p.
3, p. 12, p. 18, p. 24, p. 27, p. 30; Gianni Dagli Orti/CORBIS: p. 13;
Réunion des Musées Nationaux/Art Resource, NY: p. 13; Scala/Art
Resource, NY: p. 7, p. 10 (both), p. 19, p. 27, p. 28; Sandro
Vannini/CORBIS: p. 8, p. 22; Adam Woolfitt/CORBIS: p. 11

Illustrations: Jeff Crosby: p. 1, pp. 16–17; Lauren Fast: p. 20; Rose
Gowsell: p. 5; Robert McGregor: pp. 4-5 (timeline), p. 6 (map); Roman
Goforth p. 14, p. 15, p. 29

Cartography: Jim Chernishenko: p. 6

Cover: A detail showing a Roman woman and boy from a fresco found at
the Villa of the Mysteries, Italy.

Contents: A sculpture of a group of Roman senators.

Title page: Banquet guests at Roman feasts were entertained by dancers
and musicians.

Crabtree Publishing Company

www.crabtreebooks.com   1-800-387-7650

Cataloging-in-Publication Data

Mehta Jones, Shilpa.
   Life in ancient Rome / written by Shilpa Mehta Jones.
   p. cm. -- (Peoples of the ancient world)
   Includes index.
   ISBN 0-7787-2034-9 (rlb)-- ISBN 0-7787-2064-0 (pbk)
   1. Rome--Civilization--Juvenile literature. 2. Rome--Social
life and customs--Juvenile literature. I. Title. II. Series.
   DG77.M44 2004
   937'.6--dc22
                              2004013064
                                 LC

Published in
the United States
PMB 16A
350 Fifth Ave.
Suite 3308
New York, NY
10118

Published
in Canada
612 Welland Ave.,
St. Catharines,
Ontario, Canada
L2M 5V6

Published in the
United Kingdom
73 Lime Walk
Headington
Oxford
0X3 7AD
United Kingdom

Published
in Australia
386 Mt. Alexander Rd.,
Ascot Vale (Melbourne)
V1C 3032

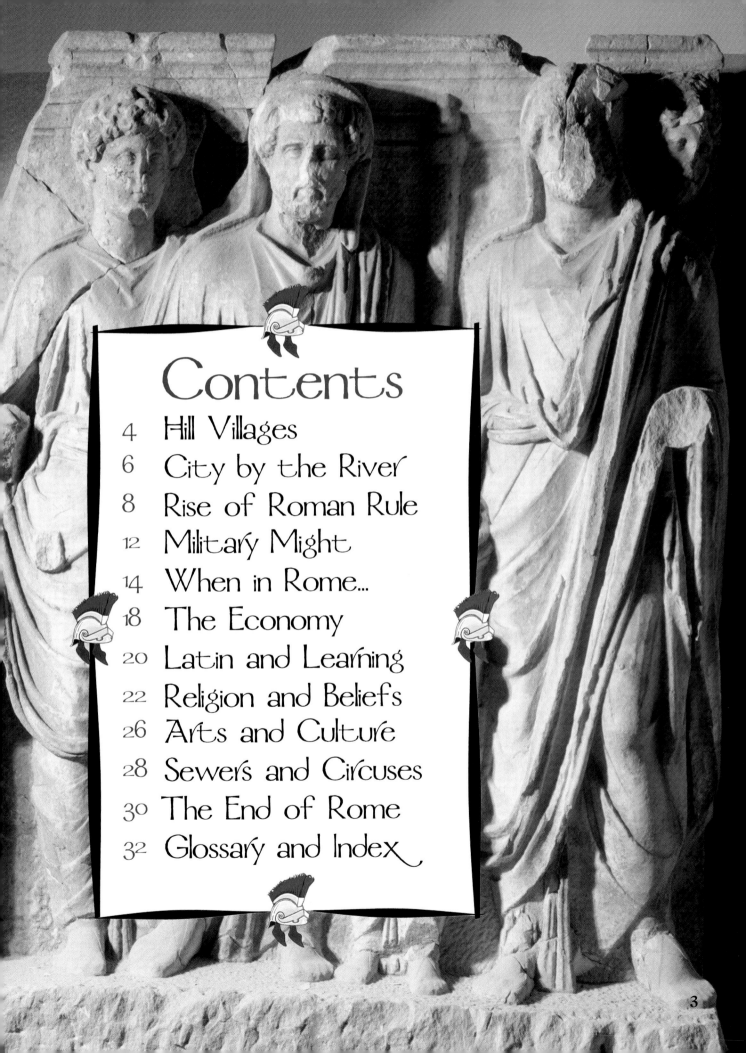

Contents

Hill Villages

The ancient city of Rome spread out over seven hills along the Tiber River in what is now central Italy. It grew from a collection of farming villages to become the birthplace of a massive empire that stretched from Britain in the west to North Africa in the south and Asia in the east.

According to Roman **mythology**, Mars, the Roman god of war, had twin sons named Romulus and Remus, with his servant. Their uncle, who feared the children would become too powerful, threw them into the Tiber River. The twins were rescued and suckled by a wolf, then raised by a shepherd. When they grew up, each founded a settlement on one of the seven hills surrounding Rome. Romulus killed Remus in an argument and Romulus' village became the city of Rome.

▲ Roman legend says that the city of Rome was built by twin brothers Romulus and Remus who were raised by a shepherd.

Etruscan or pre-Roman period: 800 BC - 509 BC	Monarchy: 753 BC - 509 BC	Republic: 509 BC - 31 BC

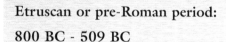

▼ Etruscan art and culture a major influence on Rome.

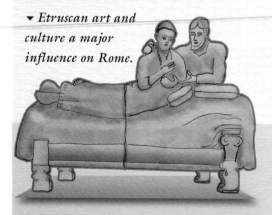

▼ Rome's legendary founders Romulus and Remus.

▸ Romans reject the rule of kings and form a republic.

Romes Legacy

The Romans built an impressive network of roads and mighty aqueducts, or channels for carrying fresh water, that crossed three continents. Rome's art, architecture, literature, and religion influenced the people who became part of the vast Roman empire. Rome's culture was also influenced by the people and cultures that were **conquered**. Ancient Rome's written laws formed the basis of the legal system used in many countries today. The Romans developed a twelve-month calendar and a system for supplying clean water to cities. The modern sports arena with tickets and numbered seats, systems for central heating, and even glass windows were Roman inventions.

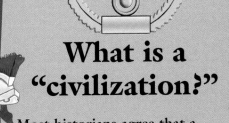

What is a "civilization?"

Most historians agree that a civilization is a group of people that shares common languages, some form of writing, advanced technology and science, and systems of government and religion.

◀ *Romans built aqueducts to bring fresh water from the countryside into the city. The massive structures still exist today, thousands of years after they were built.*

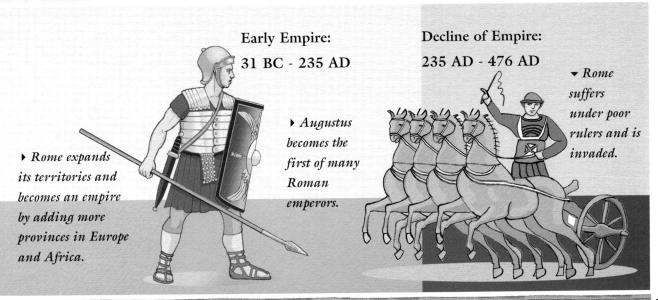

**Early Empire:
31 BC - 235 AD**

▶ *Augustus becomes the first of many Roman emperors.*

**Decline of Empire:
235 AD - 476 AD**

▼ *Rome suffers under poor rulers and is invaded.*

▶ *Rome expands its territories and becomes an empire by adding more provinces in Europe and Africa.*

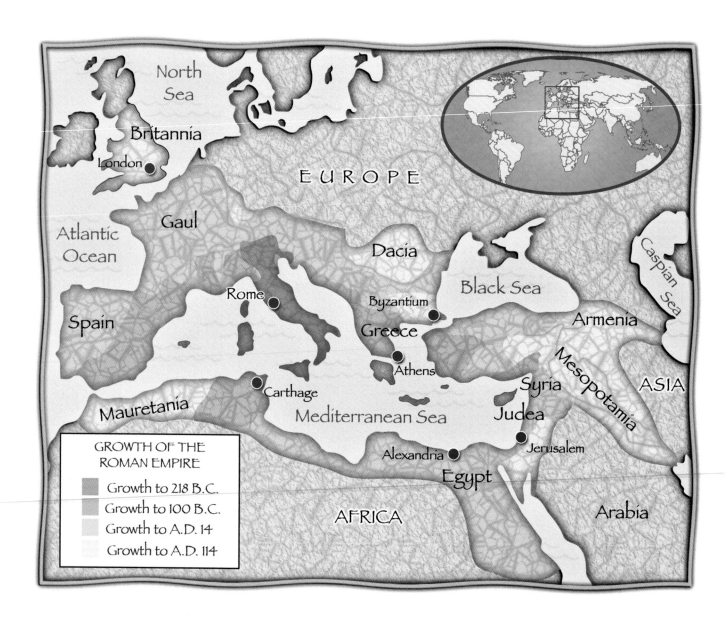

City by the River

The land of ancient Rome had fertile soil for farming, mild weather, and plenty of rainfall. The seven hills on which Rome was built provided a natural defense against invaders who wanted to take over the land.

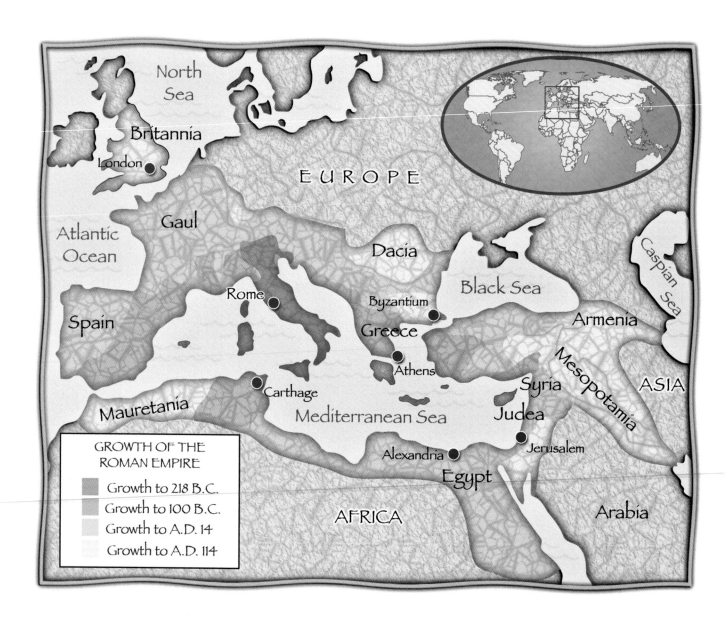

North Sea

Britannia

London

EUROPE

Atlantic Ocean

Gaul

Dacia

Black Sea

Caspian Sea

Spain

Rome

Byzantium

Greece

Armenia

Athens

Carthage

Mauretania

Mediterranean Sea

Syria

Judea

Mesopotamia

ASIA

Alexandria

Jerusalem

Egypt

Arabia

AFRICA

GROWTH OF THE
ROMAN EMPIRE

Growth to 218 B.C.

Growth to 100 B.C.

Growth to A.D. 14

Growth to A.D. 114

▲ *Rome began as a small city in central Italy and over time acquired an empire that stretched from Spain in the west, Britain in the north, Egypt in the south, and Palestine in the east.*

Hills and Valleys

The seven steep hills of Rome are located fifteen miles (24 km) from the Mediterranean Sea. In ancient times, the hills were surrounded by marshy valleys that were difficult for invaders to cross. The flat-topped Palatine and Capitoline hills were the first to be settled.

Climate

Winters were wet and mild and the summers were hot and dry. On the hillsides, Romans grew apples, pears, plums, and **quince**, as well as olives for making oil and grapes for making wine. Farmers raised sheep and goats and hunters caught wild boar and hare.

Environment

The Tiber River began in the Apennine Mountains and flowed through Rome. The river provided water for crops to grow on its fertile banks. The Tiber River emptied into the Mediterranean Sea. Romans used the river as a transportation route for trading, conquering, and spreading their culture.

Near Rome there were forests of **timber** for building and shipmaking. Stone for making concrete to construct temples, amphitheaters, or vast outdoor arenas, and aqueducts was also plentiful.

▼ *Stone remains of structures built by ancient Romans still stand on the Palatine hills.*

Rise of Roman Rule

Rome's ideal location and climate made it attractive to waves of settlers who ruled for a time, were defeated, and replaced by newcomers. Each group influenced the next through the religion, language, or culture it left behind.

The Earliest Settlers

Archaeological digs prove that the area around Rome was populated as far back as 1000 B.C. Waves of people crossed mountains called the Alps in the north and the Adriatic Sea in the east, before settling around Rome. A group, or tribe, of nomadic hunters called the Latins introduced their language to Rome. Latin later became the language of Rome.

Etruscan Kings

Around 800 B.C., a group of people called the Etruscans moved to the area around Rome. They came from Etruria, in northern Italy. The Etruscans taught the Latins their alphabet and how to make tools from metal. They built clay-roofed homes and buildings that featured curved, or corbelled, arches. The curved arch was adopted by other ancient cultures and Rome later became famous for its domed buildings. The Etruscans paved streets over Rome's swamps and built an open square called the forum at the city center. The forum was used for public events and parades that celebrated Etruscan warriors. The Etruscans expanded their territory, but by 350 B.C. the Etruscans began to lose power to the Romans. Eventually, the Romans drove the Etruscans back to Etruria.

▲ *The Etruscans were led by mighty kings. Their art often depicted battle scenes.*

▶ *The Etruscans influenced Roman art. They made statues of the gods, such as this one of an Etruscan goddess.*

◄ The Romans built cities in the areas they conquered. These columns lined a city street in present-day Jordan, once a Roman province.

Roman Republic (509–31 B.C.)

Freed from Etruscan rule, the Romans formed a **republic** in which many people held power, rather than being ruled by one king. The republic lasted for hundreds of years. During this time, all male **citizens** of Rome were allowed to vote. In the early years of the republic, only members of Rome's wealthy families were elected as magistrates, or government officials.

Making Laws

Magistrates held power for one year and helped to make laws. Two chief magistrates, called consuls, were also elected each year. They served as judges, chief priests, and proposers of law. All magistrates had to agree on decisions. Romans wanted to keep the republic free of leaders who acted like kings. In the early days of the republic, Rome's rules, or laws, were published on bronze plates called the twelve tablets.

The tablets contained laws on land ownership, inheritance, trespassing, contracts and eventually criminal laws and the punishments for crimes.

Senate and the Forum

In later years, Rome's government included senators and two assemblies. Senators were wealthy nobles who gave advice. The senate had control over whether tax money would be spent on war or for public works such as buildings and roads. Senate chambers, where the senate met, law courts, and public meeting places were arranged around the forum. The forum was like a town square with many buildings, including temples, speakers' platforms, and libraries. During the republic, Rome expanded its territory, and added new **provinces** by going to war with neighboring lands. Rome conquered all of Italy and parts of western Europe, including areas of what today are Spain, France, and Africa.

The End of the Republic

The Roman Republic survived through a **civil war** and a number of **dictators** who murdered their opponents to gain wealth and land. The Republic finally ended in 44 B.C. when a group of senators stabbed and killed Gaius Julius Caesar. Julius Caesar was a Roman army general and consul who became a dictator and ignored the rules and laws of the Republic. After Caesar's death, several generals fought each other for power. Rome's citizens rebelled and another civil war broke out.

The Early Empire (31 B.C.–235 A.D.)

The war and unrest continued until Julius Caesar's friend and co-consul Mark Antony made a deal to rule the Roman empire with Caesar's adopted son Gaius Julius Caesar Octavianus, called Octavian. Until 31 B.C., they ruled different parts of the empire. Octavian then defeated Antony and with the senate's approval ruled the empire alone. Octavian took the name Caesar to honor his adopted father. He is also known as the emperor Augustus. Under Augustus, Romans saw the beginning of a century of peace and stability, called the Pax Romana.

▸ *A statue of Octavian, who renamed himself Caesar Augustus.*

▾ *Roman dictator Julius Caesar was assassinated on the senate floor in March, 44 B.C. Sixty Roman senators took part in his death. They felt Julius Caesar was preparing to be king.*

▲ *Hadrian built a defensive wall in England in 122 A.D. that still stands today.*

Emperors Good and Bad

After Augustus' death, he was replaced by a series of 90 emperors over 500 years. Some of those emperors were clever leaders. During Claudius's reign (41 A.D. to 54 A.D.) the empire expanded to include Britain. Claudius was also a writer and historian. His wife poisoned him so her son Nero could become emperor. Born in Spain, Trajan (98 A.D. to 117 A.D.) was the first emperor to come from Rome's provinces. Trajan set up a program to give money to poor children, called the *alimenta*. He built roads, bridges, and aqueducts in the Roman provinces. During Trajan's reign, the Roman army expanded the empire to its furthest reaches. Some emperors were poor leaders who spent time plotting the deaths of **rivals**, including family members. Emperors Caligula and Caracalla ordered the murder of so many people during their reigns that they were thought to be insane. Both were **assassinated**.

Decline of the Empire (235 A.D.–476 A.D.)

During the reign of Hadrian (117 A.D. to 136 A.D.), Rome's territory began to shrink. Hadrian constructed walls along Rome's farthest borders to keep out **invaders**. Rome's mighty army began to lose battles to **barbarian** invaders in some of its provinces. Under Emperor Marcus Aurelius, whose reign lasted from 161 A.D. to 180 A.D, a **plague** spread through Rome's provinces in Europe. The plague killed many Romans and weakened the army. Rome was no longer conquering rich lands to add money to its treasury. The empire became too large to govern and control. The slow decline of Rome ended in 476 A.D.

▶ *Trajan's column in Rome is decorated with scenes of Roman battles.*

Military Might

The Romans conquered people and lands by building and keeping a strong, well-trained army. As Rome gained power, it became an unstoppable force.

The Army

Rome had an army of about 30 legions. Each legion had from 5,000 to 8,000 men. The legions were divided into different groups. This army of 450,000 men policed an amazing 1,700,000 square miles (4,400,000 square kilometers).

Ordinary foot soldiers were called legionaries and a group of soldiers on horseback was called a cavalry. Just above the rank of legionaries, were veterinarians, doctors, and musicians.

Commitment to Duty

The life of a foot soldier was tough. Legionaries marched 20 miles (32 km) a day in thick leather jackets or, if they had money, in armor made from sheet iron and wire. They carried a shield, food, and a javelin or sword. Soldiers stayed in the army for 25 years, if they survived that long. They were given land after their 25 years of service.

◀ *This fresco, or wall painting, shows a Roman soldier in a cloak and sandals.*

Great Battles

The Romans discovered horses' natural fear of elephants at the Battle of Heraclea. When the mighty Greek king Pyrrhus sent his elephants against the Roman cavalry in 280 B.C., their horses panicked, turned around and drove into their own legionaries. Rome lost 7,000 men, Pyrrhus lost 4,000. In a second battle, the loss of life was equally great. Rome eventually defeated Pyrrhus, leaving Rome in control of all of Italy. This brought Rome into conflict with Carthage, the nation that controlled the Mediterranean.

Punic Wars

The first of three wars against **Carthage**, called the Punic Wars, began in 264 B.C. It was fought mostly at sea where Roman legionnaires boarded enemy ships and fought hand-to-hand on the decks of Carthaginian warships. In the third Punic War, 100 years later, Rome destroyed Carthage, plowed the land under and sowed it with salt, turning it into a wasteland. The Carthaginians were sold into slavery.

◀ *A Carthaginian breast plate.*

▼ *The Carthaginians used elephants to cross the Alps into Italy.*

When in Rome...

The emperor and wealthy nobles, called patricians, controlled most of the land, the army, and the slaves. Poor people, called plebeians, were uneducated and did not own land.

Those Who Ruled

The patricians were the upper class of Roman society, including priests, army officers, and government. The 300 senators who ran the empire came from this class. The equites were businessmen who were not as wealthy as patricians but rich enough to own a ship for overseas trade. Those not involved in overseas trade supervised the building of temples or aqueducts, or owned shops.

Plebs and Ordinary Folk

The plebeians were farmers, artisans, doctors, fishermen, stonecutters, or shopkeepers. Some plebeians were gladiators who fought wild beasts in the arena, or drove chariots at the circus, an outdoor racetrack. Clients were poor plebeians who received daily handouts from wealthy men. In return, clients greeted their patron each morning and promoted his good name around the town.

Slaving Away in Rome

The lowest class in Rome were slaves. Slaves were usually captured in war and had no rights in society. They worked for no pay and little food until they were too sick or old to work and were then abandoned. Those who did construction or dug mines had it the worst.

Roman emperor

Patrician

Roman patricians, patrons and senators

Gladiator

Foot soldier

Servants and slaves

A woman could not own land or vote. She was responsible for supervising the household.

Family Life

The family was the center of Roman society. The father, or paterfamilias, was like a king. He had contol and power over all his children as long as he lived. A father decided how his wife, children, grandchildren, clients, and slaves lived.

Roman children were raised to be healthy and strong so they could grow up to farm and fight to defend Rome. Fathers decided if newborn babies would be accepted into the family. Babies who were ill or deformed were often abandoned in a public place. If they survived, they usually became slaves.

Clothing

Men, women, and children, rich and poor, wore wool or linen tunics. Tunics are simple, short-sleeved, ankle-length garments that were slipped on over the head. In cooler weather, a cloak was worn on top. Patricians draped a huge cloth in folds, called a toga, around the body. Senators wore a crimson stripe on their togas from shoulder to hem so they stood out. Gold jewelry was popular for the wealthy. Women often had their ankle-length tunics and cloaks colored or patterned. They carried parasols and fans in their hands. On their feet, they wore shoes of light, flexible leather. Soldiers and workmen wore thick-soled sandals.

A patrician woman's summer tunic was made from dyed linen.

Servants and slaves wore rough-hewn garments and woolen cloaks to keep warm.

Roman Feast

Bread, olives and olive oil, onions, and wine were staple foods for most Romans. Wealthy Romans sometimes attended banquets called *cenas* where they ate well and were sometimes entertained by musicians and dancers.

1. Roman banquet food included olives, eggs, meat, chicken, seafood, fruits such as figs, and honeyed wine to drink.

2. Banquet guests reclined on three couches while they ate. Often when women were present, men ate sitting up.

3. Dancers, who were often slaves, sometimes entertained guests while muscians played music.

4. Patricans dined in the spacious villas that were their homes. A dining room, called a triclinium, had fresco-painted walls and colorful tiled floors. Poor Romans lived in overcrowded apartments and often ate meals they purchased in shops. They rarely ate meat.

5. The most popular flavoring for Roman meals was *liquamen*, a salty sauce made from fermented fish.

The Economy

Fertile farmlands in Egypt and North Africa provided food for a vast trading empire, and Rome was its center. Rome's shops displayed ostrich feathers from Egypt, wine from Portugal, cotton and silk from India and China, multicolored marble from North Africa, and fish from the Black Sea.

Making a Living

The streets of Rome were busy with traders and shoppers. Shops sold perfume, paint, rope, books, and herbs. Carpenters, butchers, harness makers, and stonecutters all set up shops in Rome's streets. Cargoes of marble, wood, granite, and brick from the colonies were unloaded at the seaport of Ostia and shipped up the Tiber to the city. Olive oil used for lamps, cooking, and in soap, was Rome's most important product.

▼ *The poor received free admission to the circuses during Claudius' reign.*

Bread and Circuses

Life in Roman cities was not always easy. When the Roman army returned from wars, they brought back prisoners as slaves from the colonies. Slaves replaced plebeians in many jobs, making it hard for plebeians to earn a living. Roman soldiers often returned home from battle to find their farms in ruins because no one had looked after them, and were forced to move to the city. In 41 A.D., during the reign of Claudius, Rome's poor and hungry were given government charity. They received free grain and admission to the **circuses** or theaters.

Barter and Currency

Early Romans used a system of trade where cattle was exchanged for goods such as furniture, armor, or a horse. This trading method was called the barter system. The Latin word for money, *pecunia*, comes from *pecus*, the word for cattle. Romans bartered with cattle until 268 B.C. when the first coins were made in silver and bronze. The coins had a set value and made trading across the empire easier.

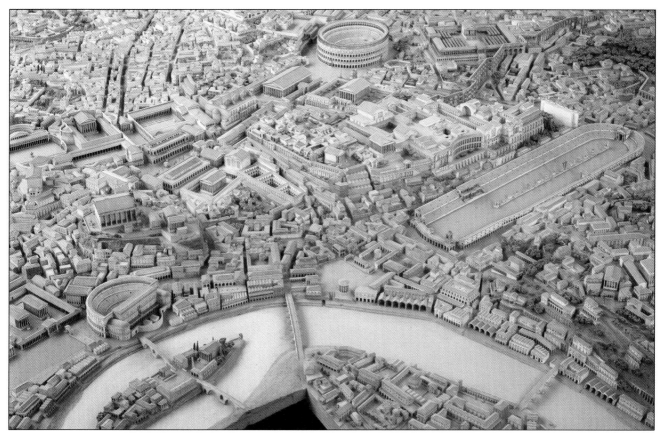

▲ *A scale model of ancient Rome shows the Tiber River winding through the city. The Circus Maximus, where chariot races took place, is the oblong stadium on the right. The Colosseum is the round building in the center.*

The Salt Road

Salt was so valuable to ancient peoples that it was used as a trade item and a form of payment. Salt was needed for preserving meat and fish before it rotted in the hot weather. The Roman government controlled the production of salt and kept the price low. Salt was collected from the sea or dug from underground mines throughout the empire. Roman legionaries were paid their wages, or salary in salt. The Latin word for salt is *salaria*.

▶ *Romans built roads as straight and flat as possible, paying little attention to who owned or used the land that the roads cut through.*

Latin and Learning

Education was important to Romans because it trained children to obey orders. Obedient children were thought to be more loyal to Rome and Roman beliefs.

Education System

In early Rome, parents taught their children at home. Children were taught by their mothers until they were about seven years old. They learned math, reading, and writing. After age seven, girls were taught how to run a household and boys learned their father's trade, were given tutors, or went to a local school. At school, boys memorized tables of measurement, including length, liquid measure, area, and money. Pupils copied the writings of Latin authors onto wax writing tablets using a sharpened stick called a stylus.

Higher Education

At age twelve, some boys went on to higher education. Sons of patricians who wanted a position in government needed to learn how to deal with people and influence their opinions. Some boys studied military strategy, so they could be officers in the Roman army. At fifteen, boys officially became men and put on the toga of manhood. A young man was then sent to study with his father's patrician friends before entering the military at age seventeen.

◄ *Roman boys work on their writing. Girls attended school up to age seven, while wealthy boys attended school afterward.*

▲ *Roman arithmetic was difficult because numbers were represented by letters. For calculations requiring multiplication and division, they likely used pebbles in a row, like an abacus.*

Language and Writing

Latin, the language of the Romans, survived long after the fall of the empire. Latin continued to be used in churches, courts, and universities as a language of religion and learning. Latin **slang** developed into modern languages such as Italian, French, and Spanish.

Calendars and Mathematics

In 46 B.C., Emperor Gaius Julius Caesar improved the twelve-month Roman calendar. This calendar, called the Julian calendar, was based on the studies of Egyptian astronomers. The month of July was renamed in Julius Caesar's honor, since it was the month he was born. March was named after Mars, the god of war. August was named after Emperor Caesar Augustus.

Is Latin a Dead Language?

The Roman alphabet is the basis for the alphabet used by many modern languages. The letters J, U, and W were added after the fall of the empire. The other 23 letters were the same as the upper case letters in the alphabet today. Many words in modern English are closely related to Latin words. For example: *Vendo* means "I sell" in English. A person who sells things is a vendor. *Video* means "I see" in English. A video is a movie on tape. *Liber* means "book" in English. Books are borrowed from the library.

Religion and Beliefs

Romans worshipped gods and goddesses who they believed controlled different parts of their lives. They created sculptures and temples for these gods and held festivals in their honor.

Household Numina

The early Roman religion was based on a belief in invisible spirits, called numina. There was a numen for everything, including the home, mountain, lakes, the day, and the night. Each family had its own numina. The numina Vesta ruled over the hearth fire. Lares was the numina who guarded the home and farm. The penates were gods of the pantry where food was stored. The paterfamilias prayed to the gods on behalf of his wife, children, and slaves.

▲ *The Pantheon is a temple dedicated to the Roman gods.*

▸ *A bronze sculpture of a numina.*

From Greek to Roman

Historians believe the Etruscans taught the Romans to worship gods whose works could be seen, such as the god of the hearth, and to make statues of them. The Etruscans were believed to have introduced the Greek gods and goddesses to the Romans. When Romans adopted Greek gods, they changed the names. The Greek god Zeus became the Roman god Jupiter, who was the king of the **immortals** and ruled the sky. Aphrodite became Venus, goddess of love. The Romans added more gods to this group of many gods, called a pantheon. They also adopted the gods of the people they conquered or traded with. Romans worshipped the Egyptian goddess Isis. In Egypt, Isis was the goddess of nature. In Rome, Isis became a mother goddess and many temples were dedicated to her. The Persian god Mithras was also worshipped by Romans in bloody ceremonies where bulls were sacrificed.

A reclining statue of Mars, the Roman god of war.

The Gods and Goddesses

The pantheon was the entire family of gods, each playing a different role in the lives of human beings. These gods were human in form and emotion and they had human adventures. Romans made a deal with their gods—if you do something for me, I will do something for you. Roman generals gave offerings to Mars, god of war, in hopes of winning battles. Young brides made offerings to Juno, the goddess of women and marriage, when they wanted to have a healthy baby.

The sacred fire of Vesta was enclosed in a round temple in Rome. The fire of Vesta was never permitted to go out, for fear that terrible evil would come to Rome and its citizens. A vestal was a girl from a powerful family, chosen between the ages of six and ten, who promised to guard the fire for 30 years. If she broke her promise by marrying, she was buried alive in an underground chamber.

Power of the Gods

Romans prayed to please the gods, who could cause storms at sea, withhold the rains, or make sure a hunt was successful. They were afraid of angering the gods through their words or actions, so they took care to build temples for them and to hold elaborate annual festivals in their honor, such as the Saturnalia held in December. At this carnival, slaves were free for the day and their masters served them, instead of the other way around.

Venus: Goddess of Fields and Gardens

Mercury: God of Merchants

Venus was a Roman goddess and daughter of Jupiter, king of the gods. Venus was known as Aphrodite in Greece where she was the goddess of love and beauty. The Romans adopted her as their own. She became a goddess of fields and gardens and the wife of Vulcan, god of fire. Venus was charming and radiant and had many children, including Cupid. Romans gave Venus' name to the planet Venus, which loomed brightly in the night sky.

Mercury was the Roman god of merchants. In statues and art, he was often shown holding a purse, because he was thought to help people in business. Mercury wore winged sandals or a winged hat to help speed him on his errands. The Romans honored him with a festival held on May 15. Named after the fast-moving Roman god, the planet Mercury orbits the sun more quickly than any of the other planets in the solar system.

Spread of Christianity

By 100 A.D., a new religion called Christianity spread through the empire. Christianity followed the teachings of Jesus Christ. Jesus lived in the Roman province of Palestine and was put to death by its governor, Pontius Pilate, around 30 A.D. Christianity's followers, or Christians, believed Jesus was the son of God. They refused to worship Roman gods. The Romans believed Christianity was dangerous and a threat to the empire. For nearly 200 years, Christians were imprisoned, tortured, or killed by the Romans. Some emperors tried to destroy Christianity by burning churches and outlawing its worship. The more Christians that were killed, or martyred, the faster the religion seemed to grow. In 313 A.D., Roman Emperor Constantine converted, or changed his religion, to Christianity after having a vision on a battlefield. Almost 70 years later, the Emperor Theodosius made Christianity the official religion of the Roman Empire.

▲ *Romans built shrines to gods in their homes.*

▼ *Modern Christians visit the catacombs, or underground burial places, for the early Christians in Rome. Christians were buried instead of cremated like other Romans.*

Arts and Culture

Romans adopted the arts and ideas of other peoples, especially the Greeks. They created literature and poetry, but were most famous for orations, or speeches.

Sculpture, Painting, and Mosaics

The Etruscans were expert sculptors and many of their clay and bronze sculptures of gods and people survive today. Roman sculpture borrowed its style from the Etruscans and the Greeks who the Romans admired. Roman statues were elegant and muscular, like Greek statues. During the republic, the Roman patricians decorated the floors of their homes with mosaics. Mosaics are tiny pieces of glass, marble, or gem, set in colorful designs in cement. Public baths were also decorated with mosaics and paintings.

Walls of temples and homes of the wealthy had colorful frescoes on walls. Frescoes are paintings applied directly onto wet plaster. The paint dried on the plaster, leaving works of art that lasted for centuries. Frescos depicted mythical animals or gods. Frescoes in private homes were often realistic portraits of the owner and his family.

▶ *Mosaics were intricate and took time to plan and make.*

Metalwork and Pottery

Roman **artisans** used a pottery wheel to coil long, thin strips of clay to form bowls and jugs. The coiled pottery was made smooth before being baked, or fired, in an oven called a kiln. Romans used pottery for serving dishes such as plates and bowls. During the Roman empire, there were several pottery factories in Italy, France, and Spain where the clay was pushed into plaster molds that formed dishes with decorative designs. The red clay dishes were sold all over the empire.

Philosophy and Writing

Romans adopted ways of learning, called philosophies, from Greece and other empires they conquered or traded with.

◄ Cicero was an orator, or great speaker, who made many famous speeches in the Roman senate.

Roman men, young and old, studied different philosophies in schools. Sometimes, Rome's emperors thought the philosophies were dangerous because they made people question the emperor's power or decisions he made. Rome had many writers and poets who were philosophers. Seneca was a writer and philosopher who wrote about maintaining order and the rule of wise people. His views got him into trouble with emperor Claudius, who **banished** him from the senate. The poet Virgil wrote a massive twelve volume poem called the Aeneid. The Aeneid was a history of the first settlers of Rome. The writer Ovid wrote books about the gods, and Horace wrote long poems called satires which made fun of Roman society. The works of many famous Roman authors and poets survived and are still studied today.

Reporting From a Volcano

In 79 A.D., a volcano on Mount Vesuvius in Italy erupted with such force that it destroyed Pompeii, a coastal town south of Rome. Roman writer and historian Pliny the Elder died while leading a rescue party to Pompeii. Accounts of his death were written in the record of the loss of Pompeii. Debris and ash totally buried the town, including its forums, temples, baths, theaters, and homes. The ash protected the ruins for years. Archaeologists began excavating Pompeii in 1748.

▲ A mosaic found at the entrance to a home in Pompeii, reads "cave canem," or "beware of the dog."

Sewers and Circuses

The Romans were great builders and inventors. They built temples, baths, tunnels, and an amazing 53,000 miles (85,300 km) of roads throughout the empire. Some Roman constructions were so well built that they are still used today.

Cloaca Maxima

The cloaca maxima was Rome's main sewer system built to drain marshlands between the Palatine and Capitoline hills. At first, the sewer was just a group of brick-lined open channels. Roman engineers enclosed the channels so they ran beneath roads and buildings. About 200 million gallons (90 million liters) of water flowed through the cloaca maxima every day.

Channels for Water

Over time, eleven aqueducts, or channels, carried water to the city of Rome for drinking, washing, flushing the sewer systems, and even for filling the emperor's fish ponds.

▲ *The cloaca maxima, or main sewer is still used by Romans today.*

Aqueducts

The word aqueduct comes from the Latin "aqua," or water and "ducere," meaning to lead. The aqueducts carried water to Rome from mountain springs as far as 30 miles (48 km) away. Some aqueducts went through tunnels in the mountains; others were buried or were ground-level covered channels. The raised channels were held up by as many as three tiers, or levels, of arches resting on columns.

◄ *A three-tiered aqueduct.*

Arches and Architecture

The Romans were known for constructing buildings with arches. They adapted the corbelled arch from the Etruscans and made it strong enough to hold tons of cement and entire stories of buildings. Roman buildings were made from concrete, a mixture of bits of broken stone or brick, with sand or gravel, cement, and water. Some buildings took years to finish. The Colosseum was a 50,000-seat arena where public events such as gladiator competitions and executions were held. Construction on the Colosseum began in 70 A.D. and ended 25 years later. The Circus Maximus was an enormous colosseum where chariot races were held.

Circus Maximus

There were other circuses in Rome and the empire but the Circus Maximus was the biggest. Romans also built spectacular buildings for worshipping their gods. The Pantheon, a round building housing statues of all the Roman gods, had walls that were 200 feet (60 meters) thick. Its dome was almost 150 feet (46 meters) around.

▼ *The Colosseum hosted fights between gladiators, between men and animals, and even mock seas battles, when Emperor Titus flooded it with water. Spectators brought their own cushions for seats and often arrived before dawn to line up for events.*

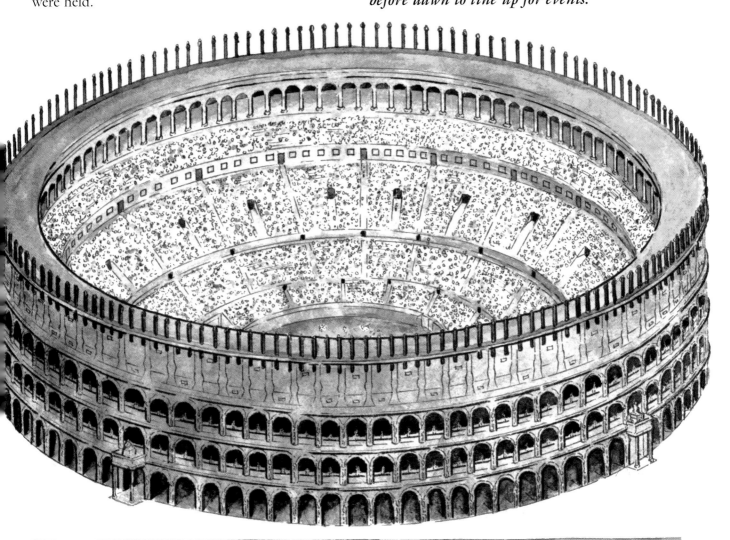

The End of Rome

▲ *A Roman frieze depicts a battle with barbarians who entered the city.*

▼ *The plague killed many Romans in 167 A.D. and may have helped bring an end to the empire.*

The Roman empire lasted for 1,500 years. Its influence and power spread through half the world. The end of the empire came after years of poor government, disease, and invasions by neighboring peoples.

Troubles Within

Hundreds of thousands of people lived in Rome, most of them in crowded slums. A housing shortage, along with crime in the streets and soaring rents, meant that the ordinary person lived a life of misery. Unemployment was a serious problem. Things became worse when farm families flooded into the city. Food brought in from the colonies was sold at lower prices than the crops grown around Rome, so farmers did not make enough to survive. The economy was further weakened when returning soldiers brought the plague to Rome in 167 A.D. The plague killed about 2,000 people a day.

Despots and Distractions

Many of Rome's rulers were **despots**, who used Rome's senate to pass laws that benefitted only the emperor's family and other patricians' families. Rome's rulers offered entertainment in the arenas, such as bloody gladiatorial competitions, to distract Rome's unemployed and unhappy citizens. With poor and weak rulers, Romans lost faith in their government and empire.

Civil Wars

Between 200 A.D. and 300 A.D., no single Roman emperor lived long enough to command the army and successfully push back the barbarians, a group of people who fought for control of Rome's territories. The empire had 23 rulers in 100 years, only one of whom died of natural causes. When Diocletian ruled at the end of 300 A.D., the empire was 1,000 years old.

The End is Near

Diocletian decided the empire would be easier to manage if it was split in two. He created an eastern and a western empire. In 330 A.D., Emperor Constantine, a Christian, declared that Constantinople, in present-day Istanbul, Turkey, was the new capital. The city of Rome was no longer the control center of the empire for which it was named. Rome's last battle was on its own turf. A Germanic chieftain named Odoacer **deposed** the last western emperor of Rome in 476 A.D. The once great Roman empire was no more.

▼ *Christianity became the religion of Rome when the Emperor Constantine converted in 330 A.D. In this mosaic, emperor Justinian and emperor Constantine make offerings to Jesus Christ and his mother Mary.*

Glossary

archaeological Having to do with the science of archaeology, which studies past human life through fossils, monuments, and tools left by ancient peoples

artisan A person who has skill in making a particular product, such as pottery or jewelry

assassinate To murder an important person in a surprise attack

banish Forced to leave a country or other place

barbarian People from outside of Rome who were thought to be savage or primitive

Carthage An ancient city in North Africa

circus Large arenas where public events such as gladitorial contests took place

citizen People who live in a city, town or country who give their loyalty to its government and are protected by it

civil war A war between two groups from the same nation or state

conquer To defeat

deposed Removed from office

despot A ruler with absolute power and authority who often uses that power in a cruel and unfair way; a dictator

dictator A ruler with absolute power and authority who often uses that power in a cruel and unfair way; a despot

empire One political unit that occupies a large region of land and is governed by one ruler

immortal Those who do not die; the gods

invader A person who enters by force as an enemy

mythology The collection of stories having to do with gods and goddesses

plague A serious and deadly disease that is often spread to humans by infected fleas and carried by rats

provinces A country or region brought under the control of the Roman government

quince A kind of fruit that looks like a yellow apple and is used to make jelly

republic A state or system of government where power rests with citizens who vote for their leaders

rivals Enemies

slang Informal vocabulary made up of invented or changed words, and exaggerated or funny figures of speech

timber Wood used for building things

Index